6-S Trouble-free Playground

Curt Hinson, Ph.D.

PE Publishing Co.
237 Beau Tree Drive
Wilmington, DE 19810
302-475-6025

Hinson, Curt, 1959-
   6-Steps to a Trouble-free Playground
       Includes bibliographical references

ISBN: 0-9658988-1-4

Copyright © 2001

All rights reserved. Any reproduction or utilization of this work in any form or by any electronic, mechanical, or other means, now known or hereafter invented, including xerography, photocopying, and recording, and in any information storage or retrieval system, is forbidden without the written permission of the publisher.

Cover Design & Printing: Sprint Quality Printing, Wilmington, DE

Printed in the United States of America

Throughout this book the terms he, she, his, and her are used interchangeably to represent both genders equally.

To my wife, Michele

Contents

Dedication 3
Table of Contents 4
Preface 6
Acknowledgments 10
Chapter 1: Introduction 11
    What is recess? 13
    The Basics of Recess 14
    The Role of Emotional Intelligence 15
Chapter 2: The Philosophy Behind a Trouble-free Playground 19
    Principle 1: Teaching Self-responsibility 21
        Self-responsibility & behavior 23
        Self-responsibility & learning 24
    Principle 2: Nurturing Intrinsic Motivation 26
    Principle 3: Using the Inclusion Style of Teaching 27
Chapter 3: 6-Steps to a Trouble-free Playground 33
    Step 1: Teach social skills 35
        What social skills should you teach? 38
    Step 2: Change the games to make them more developmentally appropriate 41
    Step 3: Change the perception of recess from free-time 48
    Step 4: Move away from threats, punishments, consequences, & rewards 52
        Where we are in today's schools 53
        Caught up in behavior modification 54
        Extreme extrinsic motivation 56
        Why we don't need punishments, rewards consequences, threats, and other extrinsic motivation 58
        Is there a time to use extrinsic motivation? 59
        Stress and extrinsic motivation 60

What should we do instead? 62
The Levels of Behavior 63
The willingness to try something new 70
Step 5: Hold a "Games Day" 71
What is Games Day and
how does it work? 71
Step 6: Use recess as a topic for writing
and discussion 75
Chapter 4: Practical Ideas for Recess 81
Recess Time: When an how long? 83
Lining up 85
Equipment 86
Now What? 87
References 91
About the author 93
Appendix A: The Levels of Behavior 94
Appendix B: Playground Equipment List 95
Appendix C: Recess Evaluation Form 96

Preface

Welcome and congratulations. Welcome to a new way to look at, think about, and present recess in the elementary school. Congratulations because you have just taken the first step toward making recess a valuable, productive, and enjoyable part of the school day.

My goal for this book is a lofty one. I hope to change the way recess occurs at thousands of elementary schools across the nation. It may seem like an unlikely possibility, however, I feel it can be accomplished. In fact, I know it can, if enough people take the time to implement the ideas suggested in this book. What this book is not, is a cure-all for discipline problems in schools, and it certainly isn't a magic potion to be poured over students to make them listen and behave. Instead, it is a group of ideas combined together to create a plan. This plan, when followed with dedication and commitment, can help lead to a more enjoyable and productive playground.

There are no easy solutions to the problems associated with recess and playground activities. Each school is unique, with unique students, and unique teachers. What isn't unique is that every school generally has the same problems and attempts to solve them in very similar ways. Although some of the methods used are beneficial, few schools consistently derive the playground environment they prefer. Because of this, I have set out to help schools bring about positive and beneficial changes on their playgrounds. This book represents my efforts to help schools in their quest for safe, trouble-free playgrounds.

This book is part of a decade of work on teaching not just movement skills, but cognitive, as well as mental-emotional skills, through play and games. Since the early 1990's I have been creating, changing, and adapting games to help children learn social skills, self-responsibility, communication, cooperation, problem-solving, critical thinking, and other such skills through movement. The response has been overwhelming. Teachers and principals, although somewhat skeptical at first, have come to realize the powerful impact play has on learning in elementary students. Not just play for the sake of play, however. Instead, I'm referring to developmentally appropriate games and movement activities that help cultivate necessary skills and learning. As you will learn as you read through this book, play is not very valuable if it's not developmentally appropriate. Many of the traditional games you grew up with as a kid are more harmful than good. It's important to know the difference and know how and when to change games to make them more appropriate. This is a key ingredient of this program and is the downfall of other playground programs you may be familiar with. I hope to change the way you look at play and games, as well as the way you feel about them and their role in education. In an era when schools are focused mainly on creating more time for students to sit at desks and produce more written work so that standardized test scores can be improved, this program is about getting students out of their desks and interacting amongst themselves. This program is a "hands-on, get-up-and-touch-others, move-and-talk-about-it" roadmap that takes schools, teachers, and students on a wonderful journey toward becoming caring, cooperative, and productive human beings. It is a beneficial program that has worked at many schools across the country. However, it doesn't work because it's a super, fantastic, no-fail solution to problems on the playground. Instead, it works because open-minded principals and teachers have made a commitment to change their thinking and take a risk on something that goes against traditional educational beliefs. If you are unwilling to change, or if you are not open-minded to trying a non-traditional approach, then this "Trouble-free Playground" program will not work for you. Don't get me wrong, it's not a radical program in any sense. In fact, the philosophy behind this program will most likely be centered directly around the beliefs you have in regards to teaching and nurturing children. What is amazing to me is that whenever I present this program to principals and teachers they all shake their heads in agreement with its underlying philosophy. However, although their beliefs are similar to mine, the school in which they work operates under a totally opposite philosophy. This conflict causes some to eagerly change what they are doing, while others view such a change as either impossible or improbable. Their chances therefore, of diminishing problems on the playground, wither due to the lack of willingness to change what isn't working.

I challenge you to view the ideas in this book and this program with an open mind. I also challenge you to implement the ideas here with commitment and dedication. But most importantly, I challenge you to decide what is best for children, regardless of what's easiest for you, or what satisfies your needs as a teacher or administrator. If you truly want to make a difference and teach children to be socially responsible adults then you've started in the right place. This program will start you on your journey. Don't be afraid to change what you've done in the past. The only way this program will benefit you, your students, and your school, is if you risk trying it. Enjoy the journey!

Curt Hinson

Acknowledgments

My most sincere thanks goes to my family; Michele, my wife, and my two sons, Taylor and Keegan. Their support and love are never-ending.

Thanks also to the many students I've had the opportunity to work with during my teaching career. I know I've learned more from them than they ever learned from me.

And thanks to the many teachers and principals I've met as I've traveled the country presenting this program. I hope you find success on your playground and continue to use play as a teaching tool. Best wishes for continued success. I hope this book is the solution to all your playground problems.

Chapter 1

Introduction

There is a time to let things happen and a time to make things happen.

- Hugh Prather

What is Recess?

When most people think of recess, they think of a time for children to burn off excess energy so they will be calm in the classroom for the remainder of the afternoon. If you think that is the main purpose of recess, you're mistaken. Recess has many purposes but burning off energy shouldn't be a priority. Typically, the hyper-active kids in your classroom thrive on activity, and the more you give them, the more active they become. If you search for research to back up the theory that burning off energy during recess helps calm kids down, you'll most likely come up shorthanded. It hasn't been shown that kids who exercise vigorously at recess are more calm or become better learners during the afternoon. Such a theory is actually a myth that everyone has been believing for more years than anyone can remember. If you want kids to be able to focus on their work later in the day, give them opportunities to socialize with their peers in a fun, active environment. What recess really is, is a time for children to learn through movement, play, and social interaction. Its value in schools however, is often over-looked because few people understand the true importance of play in the development of children. Believe it or not, recess is just as important as any other part of the school environment, including reading, writing and arithmetic. It's sad that play and social interaction are not treated with the same importance as other skills and activities being taught in schools. As you read through this book, you will obviously be exposed to my opinion and philosophy on this topic. I hope that the supporting information I offer, can help to make you more aware of the of the magnitude recess and play have on the growth and development of children.

The Basics of Recess

If you're a teacher or administrator, you spent a lot of time in college sitting through hours and hours of education courses. You probably learned a lot about how to write lesson plans and other necessary evils of being a teacher, but you probably didn't learn anything about recess. Recess is something no one teaches you about. They just send you out there expecting you to know what to do. And, as long as you keep control of the chaos, you're basically considered successful. Unfortunately, learning about recess by trial and error is a painstaking task. And chaos control is far from what running a beneficial recess is all about. It would be more enjoyable and advantageous if someone would give you a clue on just what kids should be doing at recess. Set up and run the proper way, recess can be a valuable learning tool in every school.

During my teaching career I've had my fair share of recess duty. One thing I've come to realize is that kids generally need ideas given to them about what to play. Very few elementary kids carry around a large repertoire of games or activities they wish to play. With the exception of a few of the major sporting activities (e.g., football, basketball, baseball and hockey), kids have a difficult time coming up with games to play at recess. There are always the old stand-in activities such as "kickball" and "dodgeball." But, these types of traditional games are not appropriate (I'll explain why a little later) nor do they encourage the proper social interaction that is necessary for recess to be trouble-free. Since most teachers today played these traditional-type games as children, they have a tendency to play them with the children they teach. It's not unusual for me to see a second- or third-grade class outside playing kickball with their classroom teacher. When I do, I always ask the same question, "Why?" The most common response is, "This is what we played when I was in school." As good as that reason may sound, it's not a good reason to be playing it today. Things have changed. Education has changed (although it's sometimes hard to notice!). Kids need to be taught games and activities that help them cooperate, communicate, and build self-responsibility. The old traditional-type games are not always conducive to such learning.

The Role of Emotional Intelligence

From my own experiences in teacher education I'm fairly confident in saying that what the majority of teachers learn in college is that the three R's are the most important things taught in school and recess is a time for children to have a break from learning to burn off energy. What college doesn't teach is that teaching children how to read, write and do math is only part of a teacher's job. And probably not the most important part. Common social skills such as communication, self-control, and cooperation are not only some of the most challenging things for teachers to teach, but also some of the most important. Unfortunately, they're the most overlooked.

According to Daniel Goleman (1995), author of *Emotional Intelligence,* IQ is a poor predictor of a person's future success, while "emotional intelligence" accounts for approximately 80 percent of a person's future potential. What is "emotional intelligence?" It's a form of social skills that includes self-awareness, motivation, cooperative skills, communication skills, empathy, and self-control. Where do children learn these skills? The same place they learn almost all of their social skills, through play with their peers. That's why recess is so important. Think about this, however. Children spend approximately 4 to 5 hours of each school day engaged in the three R's, focusing nearly all of their efforts toward displaying the capacity of their IQ's. In contrast, children spend approximately 30 minutes of each school day playing at recess where opportunities to enhance emotional intelligence and social skills are abundant. Unfortunately, some schools have become factories of standardized tests. Test scores have become so important, teachers are spending less time teaching and more time assessing. Suddenly being able to regurgitate facts or information has become the sole purpose of the teaching-learning process. This type of curriculum is slowly undermining the social structure of our society. Schools and society have forgotten that children are children and not small adults. Success in learning is not about what a person can do on a test. It's about how the person lives, what they accomplish, and how they contribute to the world. But if emotional intelligence such as this is so important, why don't schools spend more time letting kids develop it? And if play is so beneficial to developing emotional intelligence, why is recess always filled with arguments, fights and teasing? The answer is fairly simple. The purpose of recess is not what it should be and the games children are playing are not appropriate.

If there is anything education does not lack today, it is critics.

- Nathan M. Pusey

Chapter 2

The Philosophy Behind a Trouble-free Playground

To touch a child's face, a dog's smooth coat, a petaled flower, the rough surface of a rock is to set up new orders of brain motion. To touch is to communicate.

- James W. Angell

The foundation for creating a trouble-free playground is centered around three critical principles. It is important to know and understand each of these three principles as they lay the groundwork for each of the six steps in the trouble-free playground program. More importantly, if you are truly serious about obtaining a trouble-free playground, it is essential that you completely believe in these three principles. If you disagree with the foundation of the philosophy behind this program, you're likely to half-heartedly implement the six steps, thus failing at your attempt to create a trouble-free playground. The three principles are not radical, earth-shaking beliefs that require revolutionary steps in order for this program to be successful. Rather, they are simple beliefs in what children should learn and how they should learn it. In fact, I'm sure as you read on, you'll likely shake your head in agreement with these three beliefs. I'm confident in saying this because all three of the principles are relatively simple. Most of all, they're based on common sense.

Principle 1: Teaching Self-responsibility

The ultimate goal of education should be to teach self-responsibility. Without self-responsibility it would be a very chaotic world. Generally, self-responsibility is one of those skills that teachers hope children bring to school with them. Thus, it is not a skill that is readily *taught* on a daily basis in America's classrooms. The key word above is "taught."

There are many teachers who remind children how to be self-responsible. There are also many teachers who take the time to explain its importance and stress how much self-responsibility is needed if classrooms are to be caring and respectful. The problem is that talking about something and explaining it over and over is not a very effective way of insuring it is learned. A better way for children to learn self-responsibility is to allow them opportunities to practice being self-responsible. The easiest and most effective way of doing this is by giving children choices and allowing them to make decisions. That doesn't mean students are given control of the school or the classroom. It means they are given control of themselves. After all, part of being self-responsible is having control of yourself.

Students should generally be self-responsible for two main things. They should be self-responsible for their own behavior and they should be self-responsible for their own learning. If this goal can be achieved many of the problems associated with schools could possibly be eliminated or at least diminished to some extent. Teachers, many who readily agree they spend more time dealing with discipline problems and unmotivated learners than they do teaching, could perhaps finally put their best efforts into teaching. To imagine a school environment where a teacher's time is spent on producing superior lessons instead of dealing with disruptions and poor attitudes seems to be somewhat of a fantasy. But, fantasy or not, it's not a reason to abandon our efforts to make it a reality.

Self-responsibility and behavior

When students acquire self-responsibility for their own behavior it means the actions they demonstrate or display are actions they choose and not the actions an authority figure has determined for them. For example, students eating lunch in the cafeteria who are asked to pick up trash left behind on the table or floor typically will say, "It's not mine." This response shows no self-responsibility for helping to keep the cafeteria clean. The authority figure in this situation, who wants the trash picked up, responds, "It doesn't matter, pick it up anyway." When the student refuses, the authority figure often attempts to threaten, bribe, or manipulate the student into picking up the trash. It would not be unusual to hear the adult in this situation say, "Pick it up or you can spend 10 minutes of your recess sitting on the bench." This response takes self-responsibility away from the student as he is now picking up the trash for the teacher rather than for himself.

I know, right now you're thinking that I need a serious reality check. How many students want to pick up trash just because it's the right thing to do? You're right. Not many. Why? It's simple. We typically don't teach self-responsibility in our schools or our culture. In fact, we accept that it's not going to happen and plan for the lack of it. Look at public restrooms for example. Have you noticed that the water goes on and off automatically? Why? Because, as a society we're too irresponsible to turn it off ourselves. Instead of assuming people are going to be self-responsible and do the right thing, we assume just the opposite. It's easier to pay more money for sophisticated technology that turns the water on and off then it is to teach people how to be self-responsible. At the elementary school where I taught for sixteen years the student restrooms were often without soap and paper towels. The reason was because the students would use the paper and soap to clog the toilets, allowing them to overflow. The solution was to do away with bars of soap and paper towels. Wouldn't it have been better to teach the students to be self-responsible in the use of soap and paper towels? Of course, but such a task would be time consuming and require much effort on the part of the teachers and administrators. Schools do not see this as their purpose. They have other things to be concerned about. However, behavior problems in schools are often a direct result of the attitude created by this lack of social self-responsibility. This problem doesn't just pertain to trash in the cafeteria and water in the restrooms. It permeates through the entire school, in the classrooms, the hallways, and the playground. It is a problem that continues to grow, affecting how students act in school and how they act in society. Schools are making a huge mistake if they don't focus on the teaching and learning of self-responsibility.

Self-responsibility and learning

When students acquire self-responsibility for their own learning it means they become intrinsically motivated to learn. Learning is a very individual and unique experience. In fact, every single person learns in a very different manner. The human brain differs from individual to individual. No two people have the same genetic make-up within their brains. Each brain has a different genetic blueprint of DNA (Jensen, 1998). To compare learners or expect them to be on the same page on the same day is ridiculous. Therefore, it is necessary not only to help students learn, but it is essential that we help them learn how to learn. I went to school for many years. I have a high school diploma and three different college degrees. I can honestly say that I've learned a lot through formal education. However, I must admit that I've learned more out of school than in school. Most of the knowledge, information, and experience I have, that is useful and valuable to me, I learned on my own. I didn't learn it from teachers; instead I learned it myself. Why? Because I have a passionate, deep-seated desire to investigate the world and know more. I am a self-responsible learner. I love to learn and I take responsibility for my own learning. I'm intrinsically motivated to learn. I have friends who are very successful in their own right, but who haven't learned anything new since graduating from school. Once they left school and got a job they figured the educational part of their lives was over. Schools are making a huge mistake if they don't teach children that learning is a lifelong pursuit. It's imperative that schools intrinsically motivate students and give them the tools to carry on learning outside of formal education. In fact, anyone who leaves school with a bad taste in their mouth toward learning (and there are many who do), are truly examples of an educational system that is failing.

Principle #2:
Nurturing Intrinsic Motivation

There are two basic types of motivation; intrinsic and extrinsic. Intrinsic motivation comes from within a person. When you are intrinsically motivated you do things because they have meaning to you. You see the value in doing them. You feel a sense of autonomy because of your effort. You sense yourself becoming a better person because you participated in the effort for your own reasons. Extrinsic motivation, on the other hand, is derived from outside a person. When you are extrinsically motivated you do things because something or someone is bribing, threatening, rewarding, or influencing you to do it. You are basically doing something because some type of reward or punishment will result at the end of your effort. The best examples of this type of motivation, in regards to education, are grades, stickers, candy, parties, and/or special privileges. This type of extrinsic motivation runs rampant in America's schools. In fact, it is so common in schools that most people don't even realize its detrimental effects. Extrinsic motivation has become so widespread that teachers who don't use it are often viewed as ineffective or poor teachers.

The Trouble-free Playground program focuses on intrinsic motivation. In order for children to learn to be self-responsible it is imperative they be intrinsically motivated. Extrinsic motivation typically causes children to rely on others for praise, assurance, and direction. Children become dependent, not independent. This program is about getting students to be self-responsible. The only way to get them there is through intrinsic motivation. Yes, it is more difficult to intrinsically motivate children. Extrinsic motivation on the other hand is relatively simple. Intrinsic motivation takes time, effort, and commitment. It is a belief that what children learn in the long run is much more important than what takes place now. Anyone can extrinsically motivate anyone else. All it takes is power, authority, and/or control. These are the very things that children who misbehave are lacking. These are the very things that destroy self-responsibility and motivation. These are the very things that an intrinsically motivated individual feels. Teachers, administrators, and schools who rely on extrinsic means to motivate students are creating a society that is destined for mediocrity; a society that believes the only reason to do something is to receive a reward or avoid a punishment.

Principle #3:
Using the Inclusion Style of Teaching

If you work in education you are familiar with the term "inclusion." It refers to mainstreaming special needs students into the "regular" classroom. My intention in this book is not to debate this issue or try to explain how to mainstream special needs students into your school or classroom. My purpose is to explain to you a philosophy, or theory if you will, on teaching.

Long before the term inclusion became a popular buzz-word among educators it was a term given to a style of teaching by the late Muska Mosston. As an educator and theoretician Mosston was unsurpassed in regards to the art and science of teaching. People who knew him said he was way ahead of his time. His ideas and philosophy on the teaching-learning process were truly remarkable. Mosston created the "Spectrum of Teaching Styles," (Mosston & Ashworth, 1990) the most practical and useful framework on teaching ever created. Mosston's work is truly unparalleled when it comes to the relationship between teacher and learner. The "Spectrum," as it is known among Mosston followers, is a series of eleven different styles of teaching. Each style is based on decisions made by the teacher, the learner, or both. The fifth style in Mosston's spectrum is called the "Inclusion style." It is a way for teachers to teach and a way for learners to learn. It is based on a philosophy that every learner can be successful when given the opportunity to work at his or her level.

The inclusion style is based on the premise of having 100 percent of the learners participating 100 percent of the time at a level that meets their individual needs and abilities. In other words, no one is excluded from learning, participating, or playing. Wow! That sounds so simple, yet schools across America are filled with teachers doing just the opposite. For example, have you ever seen a "spelling bee?" It's not an inclusion style lesson. You make a mistake and you're out. Have you ever seen the game Dodgeball? It's not an inclusion style game. You get hit by the ball and you're out. I know what you're probably thinking right now. "What's wrong with spelling bees and Dodgeball? We did those when I was a kid." Exactly! We look at them as perfectly fine because they've become so common. But think about this for a moment. The child who falls out of the spelling bee early is the child who most likely needs the most help with spelling. It's hard to get practice at spelling when you're eliminated. The child who gets hit by the ball early in Dodgeball is the child who most likely needs practice with agility. It's hard to improve your agility standing along the wall or sitting in the bleachers. I would be doing the same thing during a reading lesson if I told a student who misread a word to close her book and not read anymore. It makes absolutely no sense. Here we are as educators, trying to help students succeed, and we try to do it by eliminating them from learning. Non-inclusion style lessons and games do not promote success for all students. They are strictly for the benefit of the elite; students who are going to succeed regardless of what you teach them. Who, by the way, probably make up less than two percent of your classroom.

To help you better understand the philosophy behind the inclusion style of teaching let me give you an example of a traditional, non-inclusion game and then explain to you how I would change it to make it an inclusion-style activity. Hopefully you're familiar with the game Duck, Duck, Goose. It is an old game that is still being played in schools across America as you read this. In the traditional game, children sit in a circle and one child walks around tapping others on the head while saying "duck." When the child says "goose," the child tapped gets up and chases the other player around the circle and back to his vacated spot. The chaser wins if she tags the other player before he gets to the spot. The other player wins if he gets there before she tags him. The loser sits in the middle, often known as the "pickle pot" or "stew pot" (depending on what part of the country you live in) until the next turn is completed and a new loser is determined.

Think about this game for a moment. It is absolutely developmentally **in**appropriate. How many kids are actually playing the game? Only two at a time. In a class of 24, the other 22 remained seated on the floor, watching, and perhaps cheering, as the other two run. How many children are successful? Only one on each turn. The other player is unsuccessful. It is likely, therefore, that some kids will never win a turn, or worse, may never even get a turn. This is not an inclusion style activity. Not all of the children are participating and there is a limited chance of success for some because they don't get to choose who they chase.

Now let's change the game to make it an inclusion style game, and more developmentally appropriate. First, what is good about the game? Chasing and fleeing can be appropriate movement skills for the children to learn. And adding suspense makes it motivating. What's bad about the game? Low participation and focus on failure in front of the entire class. If we can keep the chasing and fleeing, and the suspense, but get rid of children sitting and putting people in the "pickle pot," we can make this a worthwhile game. Here's what to do:

Start by placing the children in pairs. Each partner faces the other about two or three feet apart, close enough to touch each other with a hand. Mark a safety line off about 20 to 30 feet behind each player. Each player takes turns tapping the other player (on the shoulder is best) and saying either "duck" or "goose." When a player says "duck," nothing happens. When a player says "goose," she turns and runs toward her safety line while the other player chases. If the chaser tags her, he wins and a new turn is started. If the chaser doesn't tag her, she wins and a new turn is started. Partners are switched often so the children get to play others of varying abilities.

If there are 24 children in the class, then there will be 12 games going on at once. Each game has suspense, chasing, and fleeing. When a child loses a turn, there is no focus on it because she doesn't have to sit out. In addition, only her partner knows she lost. By simply changing the way the game is played, each child is given an opportunity to be successful. The children are included in learning, playing, and participating.

Chapter 3

6-Steps to a Trouble-free Playground

Much of education today is monumentally ineffective. All too often we are giving young people cut flowers when we should be teaching them to grow their own plants.

- John W. Gardner

Step 1:
Teach social skills

Whether you want to or not, if you are an adult who spends any time whatsoever with children, you will be teaching those children social skills. In regards to social skills, children learn most of what they know by watching the world around them. Adults are role models that children learn from, good or bad, whether they want to be or not. Schools have been reluctant to formally take on the responsibility of teaching social skills. This can be contributed to several factors. First, schools claim they don't have the time, or the training to implement such a program. Second, social skills are often connected to values, thus social skill training is a job ordinarily left up to the parents and the community. Some parents and community groups contest the schools placing "their" values on children. Third, if schools were to teach social skills, which ones would they focus on? How would they be taught? When would they be taught? This idea opens up a whole new world of curriculum questions.

Social skills are pretty basic. They are the skills we need to deal with our environment and the people or things in it. There are many different social skills. However, there are some rather basic ones, which we use on a daily basis, that make up a core group of skills that the average person needs. In the elementary school there are several important ones that the children should begin to learn. In fact, the lack of a few of these skills is often the culprit of behavior problems. For example, let's try a little experiment. Stop reading for a moment and think of the worst behaved child at the school where you teach or work. Do you have the child in mind? Can you picture his or her face? Now, think about the two most prominent social skills that child is lacking. Perhaps you may have a little difficulty determining just what it is the child is lacking, but hang on, I'm going to help you. In just a moment I'm going to name two basic social skills children in elementary school need, but are often lacking. The lack of these two skills often leads to behavior problems in school. I'm almost willing to bet my house and my car that these two skills are the same ones the child you have in mind is missing. Are you ready? Here goes! Self-control and communication. Was I right? Most children in elementary school who have behavior problems lack appropriate development in these two skills. Think about these two skills for a moment and let me explain them in a little more detail as they relate to elementary school children. First, poor self-control is what gets most children in trouble. They have a hard time sitting still, keeping their hands to themselves, and being quiet or attentive when needed. Many of these children are often diagnosed with Attention Deficit Hyperactivity Disorder (ADHD). Now, this isn't a book about ADHD. Nor do I claim to be an expert on the topic. I do, however, have a strong belief based on my sixteen years as a teacher in an elementary school, that ADHD is sometimes a misdiagnosis of what may actually be a lack of appropriate social skill training. To avoid having to defend my position and get into a heated debate on this topic, I will leave it at that. Please keep in mind that this belief is my opinion and not factual information that I have scientific data to support. I believe, however, that children who do actually suffer from ADHD become much better students and school citizens when they are involved in the actual teaching and learning of appropriate social skills. Second, children have a very difficult time explaining what their needs and wants are. This can often be contributed to their inability to communicate their thoughts, feelings, or ideas in a manner that an adult understands or is willing to listen to. Many times during my teaching career when I confronted students who were misbehaving, I had a difficult time trying to get them to talk about the problem (what may have caused them to misbehave) or the possible solution (steps they could take to correct their behavior). The student was frequently frustrated, angry, or feeling helpless. The last thing they were able to do was fully explain what I wanted to hear. The expectations I had for them were unrealistic. I was basically asking a six-year old, who had only been alive for approximately 2190 days, to give me an adult-level response that would solve the problem. It was pointless for me to sensibly await such a response, especially when the level of communication skills the child possessed was not sufficient to accurately do so. In other words, I was not taking the child's level of development into account. And, as most adults do in such situations, instead of using it as a teachable moment, I used it as a lesson in demoralization. How could the child not be able to discuss it with me? Such a situation made me angry, leading me not to help the child, but rather punishing him for not having the skills he needed. Skills I had not bothered to teach him.

What social skills should we teach?

There are many social skills. Some are more important than others in the life of an elementary school student. The ones I recommend you focus on first make up the core of what is known as emotional intelligence. Emotional intelligence is in essence the term given to the mental-emotional skills necessary to deal with the ups and downs of life and the people and environments in which we encounter. These skills include; self-control, communication, empathy, cooperation, conflict resolution, self-awareness, problem solving, and decision making. Believe it or not, all of these skills can be taught effectively through games and play. In fact, play is actually the best way to teach these skills because it offers children a hands-on approach to practicing them. Let me give you a few examples.

In the traditional game of tag, where several players are "it" and try to tag others, perhaps to "freeze" them, there are several valuable skills being practiced. First, the game of tag requires self-control in regards to avoiding contact with other players in the game. It requires empathy, as the "taggers" allow some players, who may not be as fast or as highly agile, to get away from them before chasing. It requires conflict resolution skills as players must work out disagreements about whether they were tagged or not. It requires cooperation, as those that are tagged agree to be "frozen." And it requires quick decision making in terms of avoiding the "taggers." From a simple game of "Freeze Tag" children are given hands-on experience in using these skills. This is a much better way to learn than having teachers lecture students on what is right and what is wrong in respect to socially responsible behavior.

In another activity, called "Picture Analysis," children are given photographs of other children in various creative positions. For example, a photo may depict a child standing with one foot in front of the other and both arms pointed out to the sides. The children form pairs for this activity and one of the players has the picture. The other player does not see the picture. The object of this activity is for the player with the picture to verbally direct the other player into the same position as the child in the picture. This is done with verbal instructions only. Once the child has directed his partner into the position shown in the photograph, the partners retrieve a new picture and switch roles. From this activity the children learn to listen and follow directions; give feedback; ask questions; observe and relay information; and cooperate. These are all very valuable skills. In fact, these skills are essential to the development of appropriate social skills and they are key skills in the "Trouble-free Playground" program.

In the activity "Cooperative Shapes," children form groups of four. Each group is given a "Chinese" jump rope and stands inside the rope, with the rope around their waists. The teacher or leader calls out different shapes the group should attempt to create with their rope. For example, each group may be asked to form a square. This is a relatively easy task since all the group needs to do to solve the problem is stand in a square, which causes the rope to form a square. The tasks become more difficult as the activity progresses. The group can be asked to make a sailboat, a tree, or the shape of the state of Texas. All of these tasks require problem solving, cooperation, conflict resolution, empathy, critical thinking, creative thinking, and teamwork. This is a very simple activity with many valuable learning opportunities. In fact, it's often simple activities such as this that allow for the most useful learning to take place.

As you can see from the above activity examples, the learning of social skills and the development of emotional intelligence, can easily take place in the physical activity setting. This is why recess is so valuable in the elementary school. Children need the opportunities to play, interact with their peers, and move in a safe and fun learning environment. Yes, learning the three R's is important, but there's more to life (and school, for that matter) than academics. Academic ability is only a small part of what a person needs to succeed in life. Schools need to recognize this and take steps toward ensuring children are given a well-rounded education that meets their needs, not only academically, but mentally, emotionally, and socially, as well. The first step toward creating a trouble-free playground is taking the necessary measures to implement social skill training. It's the foundation for the other steps that follow.

Step 2:
Change the games to make them more developmentally appropriate

There are many traditional games you're probably familiar with that you played as a kid and still play with the children you work with today. These games include: Kickball; Dodgeball; Duck, Duck, Goose; Red Light-Green Light; Red Rover; 4-Square; Spud; and more. In addition to these traditional games, you're probably also familiar with common sports-related games such as soccer, football, basketball, and the like. For various reasons, all of these activities, played in their traditional manner, are developmentally **inappropriate** for children at the elementary school level. I certainly don't mean to criticize your efforts to involve children in games, however, if you play any of the above games, in their traditional manner, with the children you work with or if you allow the children to play them at your school, you are unfortunately doing a disservice to those children. I know, you're probably saying to yourself right now, "I played those games when I was a kid and I turned out alright." That may be true, but we also had automobiles without seatbelts when you were a kid as well as other inappropriate things. My point is, just because we use to do it doesn't mean it's OK to continue doing it. Things change. And many of the traditional games we used to play contain practices that are now considered inappropriate in regards to the physical, mental, emotional, and social development of children. Let me share with you examples of what I mean. First, if you go back to an earlier section in this book titled "Using the Inclusion Style of Teaching" I explained the inappropriate practices which occur in the game Duck, Duck, Goose. For the most part, many of these same practices are the same problems with the other games I mentioned.

Let's start with Kickball. It's a very common, and often favorite, playground game for many students. I remember playing it on a daily basis in second through fifth grade. In fact, I think with the exception of Dodgeball, it may have been the only game we played. The "traditional" game of Kickball has two teams, usually with about 10-12 players each. Typically, the way these teams are selected is a couple of the more athletic children decide to play and gather up a group of peers to join in. These more athletic children usually designate themselves captain and begin choosing from among those willing to play with them. This scenario is one of the most demoralizing and traumatic experiences in a young child's life. The idea of children picking each other based on how well they view each other's ability creates an environment of elitism, favoritism, and egotism. To be chosen last basically makes the point that you're not very good; the others don't want you; and you're not a very valued member of the team. If you're one of the players chosen early, this inappropriate practice rarely has an effect on you. But, to those who are routinely chosen last, it will live with them forever. If you don't believe me, start asking some of your friends about their experiences with picking teams as a youngster. If you come across someone who was regularly chosen last, I'm sure they will be able to enlighten you. It is a feeling they never forget. Getting back to our discussion about Kickball, notice that we have a major problem (the way teams are picked) and the game hasn't even started yet. That right there should be a red flag that indicates this game is not appropriate.

Kickball is played like baseball, with a kicking team, a fielding team, baserunning, pitching, and so forth. If you watch a game closely you will notice it is regularly dominated by the more athletically-talented children. These children kick first; they play the dominant positions such as pitcher and shortstop; and they decide what everyone else does. When a ball is kicked, these players usually retrieve it, often cutting in front of their teammates to do so. If they don't retrieve it, they often yell to their teammates to quickly throw it to them so they can make the play. What's peculiar about all of this is, the other children go along with it like it's the way it's supposed to be. This social structure is not advantageous to everyone. Actually, it's the opposite of what should be taking place. Kickball is a team game. Players have roles and responsibilities. They're supposed to work together to achieve a team goal. In a playground game of traditional Kickball it's very unlikely you'll see any of this happen. Kickball isn't an inclusion-style game. Kids stand around in the field, never touching a kicked ball. Kids stand in line waiting a turn to kick, sometimes getting only one turn in a 30-minute recess period. What is the value in such a game? Do kids really need to play this way? Can we change this game to make it better? Sure, but it takes effort, time, commitment, dedication, and a little willingness to take a risk. Besides that, it goes against what we played as a kid. It also means changing the kids we work with. Unfortunately, they're already familiar with this game, and trying to get them to play differently is a challenging task.

Before I go on with another example, let me make a bold comment. If you disagree with my above description of Kickball and it's detrimental effects on children, that's fine. You're not the first, nor will you be the last. In my travels around the country and from my earlier publications, I have heard from people who think my view on games such as this is ridiculous. The two responses I often hear are, "I played that game when I was a kid and look at me," and "That's real life, and kids need to learn to deal with it." If you feel the same way, I suggest you stop here and return this book to wherever you purchased it and ask for a refund. There's very little I can do for you in solving your playground problems. There's a saying that goes, "if you want to change the world, start by changing yourself." If you're unable to change your beliefs about such games you will have a difficult time changing your playground.

And by the way, I played all of these games as a kid too. I was the kid picking teams and controlling the game. I was athletically talented. I didn't have to live with the scars of being picked last or not getting as many turns to kick. But I often think of the kids I mistreated because I was only concerned about myself, and my own success. It's called empathy (or lack of it on my part). It's a social skill I didn't have. I certainly wished I had learned it at an earlier age.

Now, let me move on to Dodgeball. I laugh when I think about this game. It's kind of a sick humor thing, I guess. Think about it. Kids throwing balls at each other as hard as they can, trying to eliminate them from the game. As I mentioned earlier (see "Using the Inclusion-style of Teaching), anytime you have a game which involves elimination, it's a bad game. Kids should not be made to sit out of games because they failed. We don't make kids who fail at reading stop reading. We don't make kids who incorrectly add a math problem stop doing math problems. Why do we make kids who get hit by a ball go sit against the wall until the game is over? It makes absolutely no sense to me. Yet, it is done in hundreds of schools everyday across the country. In fact, Dodgeball, and its many variations, is probably the most commonly played game in physical education classes across the country. If you're lucky enough to work at a school where the physical education instructor (if you have one) doesn't play Dodgeball, consider your school special.

Dodgeball has many detrimental consequences that occur when it is played. First, it is dangerous. Kids throwing balls at each other is not safe. I know there are many soft, foam balls on the market, however that does not make it safe. I had a student a few years ago who was hit on the end of her pinky finger with a foam ball during a throwing-catching lesson. Her finger was broken in two places and she needed surgery to correctly align the bones. So much for foam balls. In addition, I always hear teachers say, "Throw at the legs, not the head." Does that make the game safe? No way! First, do kids have that good of aim? From the skills tests I've conducted over the years, I don't think so. Also, if you hit someone in their feet who is trying to run from you, what are the chances you will cause them to trip and smack their head on the floor? I don't know what the odds are and I'm not willing to find out. It's just not safe.

Dodgeball has many of the same problems as the other games I mentioned. This includes non-inclusion, elimination, and safety issues. For these reasons, Dodgeball should not be included in any school, anywhere, anytime. There are many other games that meet the same psychomotor, cognitive, and affective objectives of Dodgeball without the detrimental effects.

As you can see from my above examples, there are many games, which when analyzed closely, are not beneficial to the physical, mental-emotional, and/or social development of children. This does not mean that we throw the games out and look for new or different games, instead it means we change the games we have to make them more developmentally appropriate. Earlier I gave an example of how this is done with the game Duck, Duck, Goose. From my experiences I have found that almost any game can be changed to make it more developmentally appropriate. This includes kickball, football, basketball, soccer, and other popular sports and games. Typically, such games can be played in smaller groups, such as one-on-one or two-on-one, two-on-two, or three-on-three. Dodgeball is a little more difficult to change because throwing balls at humans is one of the inappropriate practices of the game. If you do away with this aspect, perhaps by throwing the balls at targets such as pins or cones, you aren't really playing Dodgeball per se. My suggestion on this game is to just get rid of it. I have yet to find anyone on the planet who has lived a sub-standard life because they never had the chance to play Dodgeball. In other words, we can live without it.

As you have now read, the first two steps of creating a trouble-free playground are teaching social skills and changing games to make them more appropriate. These steps are the most critical in regards to changing your playground. The social skills of children are undeveloped and immature. The games they attempt to play require physical skills over and above their development. The object of this program is to raise the level of social skills the children possess and lower the need for physical prowess in the games they play. When these two things are accomplished, social development and physical skills brought closer together, almost to where they meet, your playground will transform itself into a fun and enjoyable place.

Step 3:
Change the perception of recess from "free-time"

A few years ago I went to a local computer store to purchase a printer cable. As I entered the store I encountered a store employee walking by the front entrance. I said, "Excuse me, could you tell me where the printer cables are located?" Without hesitation the employee turned toward me and responded, "No, I'm on break." As he continued to walk away it occurred to me what had just happened. The employee had refused to help me because he was on his break, which meant he had no responsibility for helping customers. Obviously, this was not the appropriate attitude to have as I decided to leave the store and go to another store down the street. However, I thought about the employee's response and realized something interestingly coincidental to recess at the elementary school where I taught. When kids are given "free" time or time when they are less supervised, such as recess, they begin to act as if they're not required to listen and follow directions at the same level as during times when they are more closely supervised. I call this phenomenon the "Irresponsibility" syndrome, and it is similar to the computer store employee. The employee believed that break time was his to choose what he wanted to do, and nothing should interfere with his "free" time away from work. In a sense, he felt he was not responsible for anything associated with work during "his" free time. Children on the playground who perceive that recess is their free time, often push the same limits of irresponsible behavior, acting as though recess is a time for them to do what they want. Unfortunately, this type of "ego-centric" attitude causes problems for teachers and playground supervisors (and computer store managers, too!). When students perceive recess as little more than a free-for-all, it's very difficult to get them to act responsibly.

Recess in the elementary school should be an extension of the learning that takes place within the classroom. It should not be looked at as "free-time." The main purpose of your recess should not be to get the children outside and away from the teachers so that the teachers can have a break. If such a purpose is conveyed in any manner to the children, then you'll likely have a very chaotic recess with many fights, arguments, and general disrespect for authority. Children should be taught that recess is a time when they can play and learn without the constant constraints of adult supervision. However, this means they must take on a higher sense of personal responsibility and be on their best behavior. Recess should be a productive learning time where everyone has a purpose and works to fulfill that purpose. In essence it's still free time, but free time that must be used to accomplish specific outcomes.

To help change the perception of recess, students must see that its content is respected and valued. This can be achieved with each classroom focusing on two major aspects of recess: games and behavior. Each classroom should have two recess-related bulletin boards. The first one is called the "Game" board and consists of a list of appropriate games and activities the students are permitted to play at recess. The second bulletin board contains a list of behaviors the children are taught in regards to learning self-responsibility. Let me explain this in more detail.

The "Game" board contains a list of games the children have officially learned from their physical education and/or classroom teacher. Games not formally taught by a teacher, are not allowed to be added to the bulletin board. Once a game is learned, it is added to the game board list and then can be played during recess. Games not on the board are not permitted during recess. (Later, in Step 5, I will explain a method for teaching children games.) This small procedure of placing "authorized" games on the bulletin board has an enormous effect on how students perceive recess. Suddenly the students realize that there are certain expectations that are associated with what takes place on the playground. Such expectations help to change the perception students have of recess.

The "Behavior" bulletin board contains a list of behaviors the students learn as part of the self-responsibility training I mentioned earlier (see "Principle 1: Teaching Self-responsibility"). Because the teaching and learning of these behaviors is a major part of Step 4 in the Trouble-free Playground program I will only briefly describe them here. More detail will be given later in Step 4. These behaviors are divided into three categories: unacceptable; acceptable; and outstanding. The behaviors are taught school-wide with each classroom bulletin board depicting the same behaviors. The behaviors are constantly reinforced with frequent referrals to the bulletin board. This simple process of placing appropriate and inappropriate behaviors in full view and then referring to them on a regular basis teaches students there are certain expectations related to their behavior on the playground. Again, as with the "Game" board, such expectations help to change the perception students have of recess.

In the first two steps of the Trouble-free playground program I said that the classroom should be where students learn social skills and games that can be practiced and implemented on the playground. This learning should be formal and have a specific purpose. In this third step I suggest that expectations for games and behavior be outlined up front, so that students gain a new perspective of recess. To further reinforce this new perspective, students should then be held accountable in some manner for the games and behavior they exhibit on the playground. This does not mean you need rules, consequences and punishments (as I will explain in Step 4). It means simply that the everyday occurrences on the playground should be given quality attention so students see them as valuable learning experiences. This can be done by observing students playing and interacting on the playground and commenting on it; by implementing group or classroom discussions; or by asking students to write about what they accomplished on the playground. The two latter of these ideas will be discussed in more detail in Step 6, as they are the core ingredients of that step. For now the main focus is to change the perception students have of recess from a "free-time" to a "productive free-time." This new perspective will add to the level of respect the students have for recess and the adults who supervise the playground.

Step 4:
Move away from threats, punishments, consequences, & rewards

Perhaps you've heard the statement, "The mind is like a parachute, it works best when open." Before I begin explaining the details of Step 4, I want to ask you to read it with an open mind. Step 4 of the Trouble-free Playground program is often the most difficult for teachers and administrators of elementary schools to swallow because it goes against beliefs that have become so deeply embedded they appear to be the norm instead of the exception. In this section I'm going to ask you to leave the comfort zone of what you're used to and look at things from a new perspective. It will not be easy. I realize this. Over the past decade I've traveled around the country presenting this very program to thousands of teachers and principals. Although many are able to step outside the comfort zone of what has always been done at their school, many others struggle with this step. The cause of this difficulty is usually a result of the deep-seated beliefs many teachers and administrators have regarding discipline. As you read this section, try to let go of any traditional, rooted beliefs you may have and open yourself up for a new perspective. In the long run, you'll be glad you did.

Where we are in today's schools

If you walk into almost any classroom, in any school, in any district, in any city, in any state, throughout the country, you're almost guaranteed to see a list of rules the students are expected to follow. This is common practice in America's schools. In addition, there's a fairly good chance you may see a list of consequences that go along with the rules. This type of rule-consequence program is a simple form of behavior modification. Basically it works like this: Do this, or don't do this, and this will or will not happen to you. Our schools have come to rely on this type of extrinsic motivation like it is the cure-all for behavior problems, unmotivated students, and low standardized test scores. Ironically, it's not the solution to these and other problems, it's the cause. And, as we continue to utilize more and more extrinsic methods to get what we want out of students in school, we consequently begin to lose sight of their drawbacks.

Instead, we fall into the trap of dependency on extrinsic means. This dependency is so widespread and common, those using extrinsic means to motivate students are considered the top teachers who are doing special things to help kids learn. Nothing could be further from the truth. Extrinsic motivation is more of a cop-out than anything. It is, in plain and simple terms, an easy method for teachers to get what they want from students with very little regard for what the students get out of the learning. In a sense, teachers who rely on extrinsic motivation, including punishments, threats, rewards, consequences, and the like, are less interested in what children learn and more interested that their work day goes by smoothly, with little distraction.

Caught up in behavior modification

One of the most popular behavior modification discipline programs is *Assertive Discipline*, created by Lee Canter (1976). Briefly, this program calls for the teacher to create a list of rules that must be followed in the classroom. In addition, the teacher decides a list of consequences that occur, or are enforced, when a rule is broken. For example, a rule may be "Keep your hands and feet to yourself." The consequences for breaking this rule are set up in steps. The first time the rule is broken the student receives a warning by having his or her name written on the chalkboard. The second infraction calls for a check to be placed next to the child's name, which indicates a loss of 5 or 10 minutes of recess. A third infraction calls for another check and additional time taken away from recess. Continued infractions call for more serious consequences such as missing an entire recess, calling the parents, and eventually visiting the principal's office. In this program one of the goals is to avoid confrontation with the student while remaining in control of the class. Obviously, since the rules and consequences are spelled out in black and white there's little or no room for discussion. This type of behavior modification puts the teacher in charge. Students are taught to obey the teacher or suffer the consequences. One of the major problems with this type of program is that the students are not taught to be self-responsible. Instead the opposite happens. Students become reliant on the teacher to make rules and implement consequences. This takes responsibility out of the hands of the student. Many teachers and administrators who use this type of program have a difficult time seeing its drawbacks. It's as if they believe this type of discipline plan is the only way to do it and they have blinders on when someone tries to introduce them to alternative ideas.

There are other problems that also arise from this type of program. For example, it's usually the same children who get their names on the board day after day. This obviously indicates that the program is not correcting behavior. Instead, what happens in this type of program, is the "good" kids are good and the "bad" kids are bad. (I use the word "bad" here to identify kids who have difficulty behaving at an acceptable level. It's perhaps not the best word to use, but I'm sure you know the type of kid or behaviors I'm referring to.) The consequences have little effect on these two groups. Of course, the children who fall into between the good and the bad, those who sometimes need reminders about their behavior, are the only ones who remotely benefit from such a program. And, that's only if your goal or purpose is conformity. Behavior modification, in essence is a method used to manipulate, bribe, coerce, threaten, or intimidate people into doing something you want them to do. Most of the time the thing they do is for the benefit of the enforcer and not necessarily for the benefit of the "doer." It's not a method of teaching self-responsibility. Rather, it's a method used to produce conformity. Some teachers ask me, "What's wrong with conformity?" Nothing really. But at what cost do we strive for such conformity? If you desire to teach self-responsibility, then different methods must be used.

Extreme extrinsic motivation

Let me share with you a program that was used at an elementary school where I taught. It was an extremely, elaborate behavior modification program used to ensure conformity and manipulate behavior, while at the same time teach students about economics. The school was an intermediate school with approximately 900 students in grades four through six. The program required the students to carry a notebook with them wherever they went. This included the library, the cafeteria, and each classroom. The students were assigned 25 points at the beginning of each day. At the end of the week the students could use their points to purchase goods in the school store.

The catch was that teachers could take away points at anytime for misbehavior, missing homework, or any number of failures or mistakes on the student's part, including not having your notebook with you. Now, don't rush back to school tomorrow and implement this type of program. It will not solve your behavior problems. In fact, I guarantee it will make them worse.

In my classroom I had a number of problems because of this program. On many occasions students would tell me to take points away from a classmate because the classmate did something they didn't like. Several times when a student was acting inappropriately, and I said something to them, another student would grab the student's notebook and quickly bring it to me and say, "Here, take away some points." There were even students who showed up in my classroom and announced, "You can't take any points away from me today, I've already lost all 25!" These scenarios were common, but not as common as the threats that were heard routinely from other teachers. It was typical to hear teachers telling children to stop what they were doing or they would lose points. The entire school was so focused on taking away points they forgot what teaching kids self-responsibility was all about. Needless to say, it was a miserable school year for me at this school. This program went against my beliefs as a teacher so much I felt the entire school was failing every student. It was very difficult to face those children. I never did buy into the manipulative-type program. I told the students not to bring their notebooks to my class. My rebellious attitude wasn't successful in helping me to teach self-responsibility. The children were annoyed with me for not taking points away from their misbehaving peers. What I learned from this was, behavior modification is so common no one questions it's validity and no one sees its drawbacks. Ironically, most of the parents loved this program, the students loved it, and the teachers thought it worked. What's funny (to me anyway) is that if this program was so effective, why were there major discipline problems at this school? If it worked, why didn't behavior get better as the school year progressed, instead of worse? Anyone who has read about or researched behavior modification, intrinsic motivation, and extrinsic motivation, will likely be able to tell you the answer. Motivating students with rewards, bribes, threats, or other forms of extrinsic means is, at best, a short-term fix for problems (Kohn, 1993). And, at the same time, does nothing to help students become self-responsible.

Why we don't need punishments, rewards, consequences, threats and other extrinsic motivation

Many teachers and administrators feel that rewards, punishments, and other extrinsic means are necessary in order to make it through the school day. Teachers who hand out "prizes" on a regular basis are actually viewed as more effective teachers. For some reason we have this belief that such behaviors demonstrate a person's genuine sensitivity toward helping students succeed. Nothing could be further from the truth. Most extrinsic programs are set up for the benefit of the teacher, not the student. It's basically an easier way to make it through the school day without as much effort. Extrinsic rewards allow teachers to get done what needs to be done without the extra burden of having to teach children self-responsibility. It's more of an undertaking to motivate students without using extrinsic methods. Students have to learn self-responsibility and other skills in order to be motivated intrinsically.

Is there a time to use extrinsic motivation?

Have you ever tried to teach a dog a trick? Perhaps you've tried to get your dog to sit, roll-over, or stay in one spot. My guess is you gave the dog a command, waited for the dog to do it or manipulated his/her body the way you wanted to, then gave the dog a treat. After several attempts and many treats, the dog started to catch on and your training was successful. That's behavior modification, and it was effective because you extrinsically motivated the dog to do what you wanted it to do. This method is used successfully with dogs all over the world. What would be easier is if from the beginning you could just say to your dog, "Hey, Spanky, sit boy, sit." But that doesn't work. Spanky doesn't speak English, therefore you are limited in your ability to communicate with him. This is where the treat comes in handy. In addition, Spanky lives his life dependent on you. He needs you to let him out to go to the bathroom. He needs you to put food and water in his bowl. He needs you for affection. He needs you for just about everything. The only way he's getting food or treats is if you give them to him. Doesn't it make sense that he's easy to manipulate because he's dependent on you? Dogs are not self-responsible, if they were everyone would have one. Extrinsic methods are the only way to communicate to the dog what you want him to do. Children are not the same. We can communicate with them and we want them to become self-responsible and self-reliant. We have other ways to teach them besides behavior modification. Using extrinsic methods to get children to learn is, in my opinion, an unwillingness to take the time and effort to teach them valuable skills such as communication and self-responsibility. Teachers who rely on such methods are failing kids. Parents should be outraged at what schools do, but unfortunately, parents are doing the same thing at home.

Stress and extrinsic motivation

Did you ever notice how your body changes when you're in a highly stressful situation? Perhaps you start to sweat or breathe differently. Maybe you get sharp pains in you lower back or your stomach. Perhaps you have to go to the bathroom. All of these types of symptoms are your body's reaction to the stress being placed on it. When your body is put into stressful situations your brain reacts to the event by releasing hormones to counteract the stress. Release of hormones causes the body to change; affecting how a person acts, reacts, and thinks. Research has shown that moderate levels of stress are conducive to learning, while low levels or high levels are detrimental (Jensen, 1997). Secretion of hormones in the brain has a definite effect on how the brain functions. Therefore, if a person receives no stress or too much stress learning can be affected. For example, Noradrenaline, a hormone secreted when the brain is overly stressed, reduces the brain's ability to think critically, solve problems and gain understanding. At the same time, Serotonin, another hormone, is reduced within the brain. Low levels of Serotonin can lead to depression, shyness, and deviant behavior. Is it no wonder that when we threaten kids with statements such as, "You do that again and you'll miss recess today," we create problems for ourselves? Our own statements and actions actually restrict the ability of children to act the way we're trying to get them to act. In other words, it's not what the kids are doing to us, it's what we're doing to the kids.

Stress can come from many sources, it doesn't have to be from threats. Trying to compete for a prize; failing in front of your peers; being embarrassed; or simply having to take an exam, can all lead to the same hormonal problems in the brain. When we subject children to stressful circumstances we automatically inhibit their ability to deal with the situation. This can cause increased behavior problems, decreased motivation, and poor school performance. The saddest part is, as teachers we never see what we're doing to kids as the problem. Instead, we see their reaction to what we're doing as the problem. Maybe if we change what we're doing we can change the reaction. This isn't rocket science, this is just plain common sense.

What should we do instead?

It's easy for someone to tell you not to use punishments, or rewards, or threats, and the like. And thus far, that's exactly what I've done. For many of us, however, we know few alternatives to dealing with the everyday problems associated with children and the playground. We have a tendency to do or teach what we know. If we don't know it, we can't use it. That's pretty simple and I'm sure you agree. There are alternatives, nonetheless, that can help solve our problems and at the same time are beneficial in teaching children how to be more self-responsible without using extrinsic methods. My goal is to share with you an alternative way to deal with problems that enables you to move children toward being self-reliant on the playground. Nothing is more frustrating than having dozens of children run over to you and complain about how others are playing or how others are mistreating them. This is a sign that children have become dependent on you to take care of their problems. What would be better is if children could sort out their own minor problems and play in respectful manner. But because children have come to realize that tattling to an adult about others elicits a response from the adult, the tattling continues. The alternative is to teach children to be self-responsible using a system of acceptable and unacceptable behaviors. As I will discuss in detail in the next section, these behaviors are divided into three levels and the children are taught to make choices from within the levels.

The "Levels of Behavior"

If you want children to listen, behave, and stay on task, you have to teach them to do so. During my teaching career I've tried many different ways to manage behavior in my class. From trial and error I learned fairly quickly that it was better to teach the students how to manage themselves instead of me trying to control them. When I tried to place too much control over them I ended up in power struggles with kids who didn't know how to act appropriately. That's when I went in search of a method which could help me teach students to be self-responsible. I finally came across a program known as the "Levels of Behavior." The Levels of Behavior is a system designed to teach self-responsibility. The ideas that I share here are adaptations taken from the work of Dr. Don Hellison (1985 & 1995). Hellison developed his "Levels of Behavior" while working with inner-city youth in some of the worst parts of Chicago. I don't claim to be a "guru" of Hellison's work, however, in the brief conversations I had with him and from reading his work, I have come to find his ideas to be the most effective way to teach self-responsibility.

Hellison's goal was to teach his students they controlled who they were and how they acted based on the choices they made. For many of the students he worked with, the only place to go was up. What his students didn't know was that it was their choice to make that decision. He was only there to make them aware of their capabilities.

Hellison' model is based on a hierarchy of five levels of affective development. The five levels, numbered zero through four, correspond with student actions and are labeled: Irresponsibility; Self-control; Involvement; Self-responsibility; and Caring. Each of these levels contains actions or behaviors students choose or don't choose to engage in. For example, a student would be at level 0 (Irresponsibility) if he hit or pushed someone else. In contrast, a student would be at level 4 (Caring) if she helped someone up who had fallen. The purpose behind this hierarchy of levels is to show students there are different ways to act in any circumstance. The goal is for them to be responsible enough to choose the level they feel is appropriate in the situation given. Students are constantly asked to think about the level which they have chosen, and make adjustments if necessary to move themselves toward a more appropriate choice.

Over the years I've adapted Hellison's model to meet the needs of the students I supervise on the playground. In the elementary school setting I feel three levels are enough for students to comprehend, so I limit my hierarchy to: Unacceptable (Level 1); Acceptable (Level 2); and Outstanding (Level 3). To make it even more simple for students to comprehend, I usually just refer to the levels by number (1, 2, or 3). You could very easily use other titles, such as "Unsatisfactory, Satisfactory, and Outstanding." The titles you use can be something that suits your needs and makes sense to your students. It's not that important what they are, rather it's important the students understand the relationship between them and their behavior.

Under each level is a list of behaviors that are characteristic of a person working at that particular level. Displaying these behaviors puts a child at a certain level on the hierarchy. The children are taught it is their responsibility to choose the level at which they want to be involved. This helps teach self-responsibility because the child is making a choice about behavior on her own. As a teacher, you're not telling kids how to act, you're showing them what is acceptable and what isn't, and letting them choose where they want to be.

Appendix A shows an example of the behaviors under each of my levels as they relate to recess and the playground. These behaviors can be changed to meet your needs whether they be for the classroom, the hallway, the cafeteria, or the playground.

A poster or sign showing these behaviors should be posted in each classroom and referred to each time before the children go out to recess. If the children exit the building from another location, such as the cafeteria, then these behaviors should be displayed there and the person in charge of dismissing the children out to the playground should refer to the behaviors before dismissal. This is important because the children need to be reminded often about their level of behavior in order for this approach to have an impact. Simple questions such as, "Who can tell me something you can do to be at the exceptional level?" should be asked everyday prior to going outside. A good answer would be, "Allow someone who doesn't have anyone to play with come into your game."

Once you have chosen your levels and decided which behaviors fall under each one, it's time to make posters and implement the levels. First, all levels and behaviors should be the same for all classes schoolwide so that everyone knows what to expect. Next, the students should be taught what it means to be self-responsible and how their behavior is a choice they get to make. Once this is understood, students are constantly reminded to think about their level of behavior. When children choose to be involved at recess at an unacceptable level, several things occur. First, they are most likely not involved in an activity. This is not necessarily because they don't want to be or that the person supervising recess has made them sit out, but rather because their actions are keeping them from playing. For example, if two children are playing a partner game such as *Soccer Golf* (from my book, *Games Kids Should Play at Recess*) and they begin arguing over who gets to kick the ball first on the next turn, the game is temporarily stopped due to the argument. What the children need to understand is that if they had remained at the acceptable or outstanding levels and avoided the argument, the game would not have been disrupted. Therefore, the choice they made about their level of behavior has interfered with their playing. Can you see now how this program helps to teach self-responsibility? If the children want to play then they have to change their own behaviors. And with the behaviors being reinforced on a daily basis, they should know exactly what it takes to move on and continue the game. Ideally, this would be as far as any problem goes. But, in reality, I know that isn't true.

Second, the children may not be able to resolve their problem without help. It would be nice if all children could resolve their own conflicts, but like I just said, be realistic, it isn't going to happen. Therefore, the playground supervisor (teacher, aide, etc.) will be called upon to help. In this circumstance the first thing the supervisor should do is ask the children to tell her the level at which they are playing. Obviously, the children should say they are at the unacceptable level. Once they recognize this, they should simply be encouraged to solve their own problem by changing their level. The supervisor may want or need to offer some suggestions on how this might be done. In the example used above, the supervisor might suggest that to avoid arguing they should devise a method to determine who kicks first on each turn, such as, whoever kicked first on the last turn goes second on the next turn. If this doesn't work perhaps the children should find new partners to play the game with or select a new game. The supervisor could help them find a new player or suggest a new game. If this is not feasible, or possible, or if the argument has escalated into hitting and pushing before other steps have been implemented, then it may be necessary to remove the children from recess. This should, however, be a last resort, after other options have been attempted. The supervisor should avoid solving the conflict by telling the children what to do. Remember, you're trying to teach them about being self-responsible. Making suggestions is fine, but let the children make the final choice so that the decision belongs to them. Finally, when children come to the supervisor with a problem they usually tell what the other person did, or say that the other person did it first. This is often a sign that the children do not know how to take responsibility for their actions. Blaming others is common practice in elementary school. It's part of the "me first" phase children go through. The supervisor shouldn't get frustrated when this occurs. It just means the children are still in the process of learning about self-responsibility. Most children will get it, but some will not. If, after all the above has been tried, the supervisor feels the children are not capable of solving the particular conflict, then she should solve the problem and get the children involved in another activity or with another person. However, it's important to hold out and make the children decide to change their level of behavior on their own. As long as there's no threat of a fight, a small dispute is conducive to teaching children how to solve their own conflicts. Also, in the example I gave above with *Soccer Golf*, there are only two children involved. If these two have a difficult time settling their dispute it's only disrupting them and not 100 or so other children who are still playing.

At this point let me go back to something I said earlier. In *Assertive Discipline,* I said that the "good" students behave regardless of the situation, the "bad" students remain disruptive, and the "in-between" students seem to get the most out of it. In this plan, you might be thinking the same thing is going to happen. But wait a minute. There's a difference. In this program you're not trying to control the students. You're giving them opportunities to control themselves and leaving the decision making up to them. This is critical in motivating children to participate.

The idea of implementing the Levels of Behavior often seems radical to the acrimonious behaviorist. Primarily, because it doesn't offer answers or solutions to problems in black and white. Instead, it leaves a lot of gray area. This is uncomfortable territory for many teachers and administrators who are accustomed to rules and consequences. The biggest difference about this program is it's an ongoing process that never ends. In contrast, behavior modification is more product- oriented, focusing on getting what you want. Once you get it, you feel satisfied, even if the misbehaving child learned nothing from the episode. Such practices do little to help teach self-responsibility. The Levels of Behavior philosophy continuously focuses on helping students become more self-reliant. I have yet to find a school, using behavior modification methods for discipline problems, that ends the school year with fewer behavior problems than they had at the beginning of the school year. That fact alone should be an instant indicator that behavior modification doesn't help students to become more self-responsible. If you want to change the way students act and/or the way they treat each other, you have to move away from threats, punishments, rewards, and consequences. In the long run, what students learn will be beneficial to everyone.

The willingness to try something new

Obviously you're reading this book because you're having problems on your playground. What I want you to think about is what steps or measures you've taken to solve these problems. Most likely you've used the same methods day after day, week after week, year after year, expecting successful results but always ending up with the same problems. What is hard to understand is that your methods aren't working and it's time to try something new. The difficult part is being willing to let go of the ingrained beliefs you have related to discipline and behavior. The Levels of Behavior program is a new way to approach discipline and behavior. It's certainly not a magic potion to be poured over students so they magically become well-behaved. And, it certainly isn't a black and white, do this-do that, behavior package that you buy out of the back of a magazine. Instead, it's a process; a process of teaching and learning so students become self-responsible and intrinsically motivated. It's not easy and it's not fail-proof. But it's what children need if we expect them to grow up and become respectful, empowered citizens.

Step 5:
Hold a "Games Day"

In Step 2 of the Trouble-free Playground program I explained the importance of changing the games kids play at school to make them more developmentally appropriate. The goal in Step 5 is for students to learn as many of these developmentally appropriate games as possible, so they have a foundation of games to select from while at recess. The learning of these games is best done on a large scale, at one time, with the entire school involved. This not only makes it efficient but it also helps demonstrate to the students that the school as a whole, is focused on the importance of recess.

What is "Games Day" and how does it work?

Games Day is a day where everyone gets to go to recess for the entire day! Wow, just think, recess all day long. I doubt you'll have many students absent from school on Games Day. The only thing that could be better than recess all day long is having ice cream as the entrée for lunch. Imagine that. Kind of makes you wish you were a kid again. Anyway, the purpose of Games Day is for kids to learn games. The entire school is involved in Games Day and yes, it's really a day with nothing but recess. Here's how it works.

A list of games is compiled which includes all of the games the school staff feels are appropriate for the students to play and learn. (For ideas on such games, you should obtain a copy of my book, *Games Kids Should Play at Recess).* Each classroom teacher in the school selects a game from this list, which they are willing to teach to the students. Complete directions and procedures for each game should be given to the teachers prior to Games Day so they can prepare ahead of time for teaching the games. Equipment and other necessary materials for the games are obtained prior to Games Day and distributed to the teachers who need them (not all games will require equipment). A map or diagram is designed that depicts where each teacher will be located on Games Day. Some games will need to be played on grass, while others can be played on pavement. It is important to design the layout of Games Day so that each teacher has an appropriate location to teach his game. Keep in mind that safety is the primary issue when selecting space. A secondary issue is to arrange the space so that the children can move easily from one game to the next without delay and confusion.

On Games Day each teacher reports to her place, bringing the necessary equipment and, of course, her students. Approximately 5 or 10 minutes are set aside for the initial set up of the game. After the set up, the "Games" begin. Each teacher spends approximately 10 minutes teaching her game to her own class. (You can vary this time to meet your needs.) After 10 minutes, a signal is given (e.g., horn, whistle, etc.) and the classes rotate. The teachers stay where they are, while their students move onto another teacher. This pattern continues throughout the day until every class has had a chance to visit every teacher for 10 minutes, and learn each of the games.

Depending on the size of your school and the number of classrooms you have, Games Day will need to be adjusted to meet your situation. For example, if your school houses grades K to 3 and has 15 different classrooms, then your Games Day can have all 15 classes participating at once. In one hour you can cover approximately five different games. Therefore, your Games Day will take three hours to complete. I suggest you do two hours before lunch and one hour after lunch. If your school houses grades K-6 and has 28 different classrooms, then your Games Day will need to be adjusted somewhat. First, because of the wide range of grades, there are games that the sixth graders will learn that are not appropriate for first grade, and vice versa. Therefore, you may find it best to divide you Games Day into two groups; K-3 and 4-6. You can do these two groups on the same day or separate days if your space and equipment needs restrict you in any way. I suggest separate days so that your event remains manageable. It can be quite over-whelming trying to manage 28 or more classrooms at the same time on one day.

After Games Day is complete your students will have knowledge of enough games to last for most of the school year. As the year progresses it is beneficial to add new games to this list. This can be done a couple of ways. The best way I have found, and the way I suggest, is to have the physical education teacher teach the students new games. Of course, if your school doesn't have a physical education teacher this plan isn't effective. If you're lucky enough to have one, ask them to teach the children some games that can be played at recess. After the students learn a game in PE class, the PE teacher gives the classroom teacher a description of the game and directions on how to play it. The classroom teacher is then required to play the game with her class at least once. When this requirement is fulfilled, the game can be added to the Game Board in the classroom. Remember, only games appearing on the Game Board, can be played at recess (refer to Step 3). This encourages teachers to play with their students, which, as you read earlier, is one of the best ways to teach emotional intelligence skills.

Games Day is a great way to start the school year off on the right foot in regards to changing your playground. It helps students to understand that recess is important and is a vital part of the school day. The fact that the entire school is taking the time to learn games demonstrates to kids the value of play and that, as adults, we want them to play, have fun, and enjoy themselves in a safe, productive manner.

Step 6:
Use recess as a topic for writing & discussion

To help promote the importance of recess and encourage responsible behavior, it's beneficial to talk and write about the daily occurrences on the playground. When students are asked to share their thoughts about recess it gives them an opportunity to focus on a topic that is very personal to them. Recess is a place where students have ownership and control. By letting them focus on recess at times other than recess itself, students learn that recess is a valuable part of the school day. As I mentioned earlier, by changing their perception of what recess is, we help students become more responsible for their actions on the playground.

One of the best ways to encourage responsible behavior on the playground is to set aside regular class meetings to discuss recess. This can be done at anytime during the day. The key is to make it consistent so the children look forward to it and plan for it. Some teachers like to hold this discussion first thing in the morning. Others like to do it right after the children return from recess. And, others like to do it at the end of the day, as sort of a wrap up of the day's events. Again, it's important that the children have this opportunity, as it can be an exciting time for many to share their thoughts and feelings.

When holding class meetings to discuss recess and the playground, it can be overwhelming, as every child wants to talk and give input. It is beneficial to set up guidelines for the meetings to help with organization. For example, teachers may want to create a "Recess Box," which is simply a shoebox with a slot cut into the top of it. The children write comments, suggestions, or other issues on small pieces of paper and put them in the shoebox. During the class meeting the teacher pulls the messages out of the box and uses them to initiate discussion about the playground. Another idea is to let everyone have the same amount of time (e.g., 30 seconds) to comment on recess. This makes it fair to everyone as far as getting a chance to speak, however, it doesn't allow for your discussion to go off on tangents, which is actually a benefit to having the discussion. One thing to keep in mind is not to turn the class discussion into a complaint session with students tattling on each other. The discussion can be about problems, but should be directed more toward making recess enjoyable, fun, and a learning experience for all.

Aside from class discussions, another useful tool is to have students do writing assignments about recess. One of the easiest ways to achieve this is to have the students keep a "Recess Journal." This journal is a notebook students use to keep track of the things they are doing at recess. The journal works like this. Each day when the children return from recess they are given approximately 10 minutes to write in their playground journals. Since writing is a skill every child needs practice with, this is a great way to do it. Recess is real to an elementary kid. It's fun and enjoyable. It's a time where they get to socialize and be with friends. It's what their lives center around. Asking them to write about a topic that means so much to them is a lot easier than asking them to write about a book they may not have enjoyed. Writing in a playground journal also shows the children that what they did at recess is important. It also helps to motivate kids to do something productive on recess and keeps them from getting into conflicts. If you have to write about something when you go inside, you're less likely to do nothing at recess, and you're also less likely to do something unacceptable because you're going to have to write about it.

The teacher should treat the playground journal just like any other writing assignment. It should be read and evaluated in some manner. If it's important enough for a kid to write it, then it's important enough for the teacher to read it.

The entries into the journal can be simple. Asking students to write about what game or activity they played and who they played with, is the best place to start. Having the children write about their level of behavior is also important, as it reinforces the self-responsibility you're trying to teach. Whenever a child has a problem at recess, he should be asked to write about it. This is always good to have on hand when meeting with parents.

Obviously, some younger children are unable to write. Their playground journal should consist of drawings of what they played during recess. At the bottom of the drawing, they can include key words they know related to what they did during recess, or the names of the children they played with.

Another suggestion is to have students write about recess as part of their Language Arts curriculum. These writings can be: descriptive/informative (explain what you did at recess today) or creative (explain what would happen if you found a turtle on the playground?). These writings should also be treated just like any other writing assignment and be read and evaluated in the same manner. This signals the importance of recess to the children and integrates an important part of their day with a subject matter that some children struggle with.

If you're looking for a quick, easy way to involve children in thinking and writing about recess, you may want to try a "Recess Evaluation Form." This is a simple form that the children fill out when they return from recess. It takes less than five minutes in most cases, and adds credibility to the importance of recess. The form (see page Appendix C for a sample form) asks four basic questions: 1) What did you play today at recess? 2) Who did you play with? 3) What was your level of behavior? and 4) What did you do to be at that level? These basic four questions allow children to reflect back on recess and process their thoughts about what happened. It's a great short writing exercise as well as wonderful thinking task. These forms can be collected daily and kept in a folder for each child, or sent home on a daily/weekly basis so that the parents can see what their children are doing on the playground. When children are given opportunities to express their thoughts and feelings about recess at times other than recess, they learn that recess is considered an important part of their learning experience. In addition, writing about and discussing recess helps to build a more caring community among the students in a class. This in turn reduces discipline problems and makes recess a productive part of the school day. It's all connected, and once you start the ball rolling toward self-responsibility you'll be amazed at how well students respond. Children want to be independent and make decisions on their own. It's time we empowered them to do so.

A teacher affects eternity; he can never tell where his influence stops.

- Henry Brooks Adams

Chapter 4

Practical Ideas for Recess

The day will happen whether or not you get up.

- John Ciardi

Most schools look at recess as a time for children to get outside, soak up some sunshine, breathe some fresh air, and give the teachers a break. That's all great stuff, but it means that recess isn't high on the totem pole of priorities, therefore it doesn't have any clout when it comes to scheduling. Because of the lack of credibility associated with recess, little thought is put into its value. Often this leads to problems in school that could be corrected or avoided altogether with a little more respect for the value of recess.

Recess Time: When and how long?

The amount of time kids spend at recess varies from school district to school district. In some parts of the country students attend recess twice a day for 20 or 30 minutes each time, whereas in other parts of the country 15 minutes is all they get. Generally, it's beneficial for children to get at least 30 minutes of recess each day. Obviously, a little recess is better than none, but 30 minutes should be the minimum.

The majority of schools schedule their recess period immediately after lunch. This makes no sense whatsoever. Physiologically, having recess right after lunch is harmful to the digestive system. When food enters the stomach the body diverts large amounts of blood to the stomach and intestines to aid in the proper digestion of the food. When children go out and run around shortly after eating, the largest muscles in their bodies (legs and buttocks) draw blood away from the digestive system. This causes the food not to be digested properly, leading to stomach cramps and/or diarrhea. Improper digestion means children do not absorb the necessary nutrients from the food. This can lead to major complications such as low energy, inattentiveness, and inadequate growth and development. Recess should be scheduled before eating so that the digestive process is not affected. In addition, nutrients can be put back into the body after exercising, which allows for students to be more alert and attentive in the afternoon hours.

The ideal schedule would be to allow students several short, 15-minute recess periods during the day. Ideally, one in the morning, one right before lunch, and one in the afternoon, would be best. Educational critics who are gung-ho on accountability and standardized test scores would certainly cringe at the thought of so much recess time. How could kids learn all they need to know in school if they had three recess periods a day? First of all, there's already plenty of time in a school day. Tacking on extra learning minutes is not the solution to better learning or successful students. Second, many proponents of standardized tests, accountability, and other nonsense related to "higher standards" for students are not teachers and have very little knowledge about what kids should learn and how they should learn it. I'm not saying more recess is the solution to better schools and better students. I'm saying we need to take a look at what we're expecting from children and compare it to what they need and how they learn. If we carefully examine these issues we'll find schools are moving in the wrong direction.

Excellence in education should never be measured by scores on standardized tests. It should be measured by the achievements of communities and society in general. Pursuing the goal of students obtaining high scores on standardized tests will never expand mankind to the level it is capable of advancing. Seeking self-responsibility and intrinsic motivation among students will.

Lining up

Getting kids to line up after recess so they can re-enter the building in a reasonable manner is by far one of the most painstaking tasks of being a teacher, administrator, or playground supervisor. It seems no matter what you do, it's utter chaos. There are several suggestions I have, some a bit more radical than others.

What if you didn't have the kids line up? I know it sounds ridiculous, but try it. Forget all those nice little, straight lines with no one talking and everyone standing at attention. This isn't the US Marines. It's an elementary school. Why do we expect them to act like little soldiers? Just blow the whistle and tell everyone to go inside. Don't try to control the kids, let them control themselves! By the way, if you teach your students to be self-responsible then this way is the only way you need.

If you insist on using lines, don't put the lines right next to each other. Have some classes line up at the door, while others line up on the pavement, or on the sidewalk. It makes no sense to have five to ten classes lined up in the same area at the same time. You'll pull your hair out trying to get them to stand there. All you'll end up doing is getting frustrated then you'll most likely have to rely on some sort of extrinsic motivation (a punishment or reward) to get students to listen to you and stand in line quietly.

Stagger the times classes go inside. Have a signal for each class. Line one up at a time and send it in, then work with the next one. Give a warning signal that lets the students know when they have 2 or 3 minutes left before it's their turn to line up.

Equipment

Recess equipment is a problem for many schools. From what to buy and how much to buy, to how to care for it, schools have a difficult time dealing with playground equipment. It seems no matter what method you utilize equipment ends up broken, left outside, or missing altogether.

The method I've found to be most beneficial is to purchase equipment for each classroom then let them be accountable for its whereabouts. Classroom teachers should assign an "Equipment Manager." This can be done on a weekly basis or longer (longer if you come across a good one who does a good job). The equipment manager's job is to make sure everything that went out comes back in. This person reports any missing equipment to the teacher, who then can initiate a "search party" if necessary.

In Appendix B I've listed the equipment necessary for the typical classroom of 20-30 students. This package generally costs just under $100 per classroom for the year. You can certainly spend less than this, but you'll limit the activities kids can get involved in during recess. Recess equipment is a necessary evil. It's not cheap and it doesn't last too long, but it's certainly necessary and beneficial.

Because most playground equipment needs to be replaced each year, it's a reoccurring expense. It's better to buy quality equipment and re-use what's still in good shape the next year. Principals should look at the cost of playground equipment as a good investment in the development of children. Equipment should be developmentally appropriate and safe for the children using it. For example, first graders should not be playing with regulation size and weight basketballs. If they do, you're sure to have someone hurt. When they throw the ball up at the basket and miss (which will occur most of the time), someone underneath the basket will get hit in the face. It happens all the time, trust me. Having good, quality equipment shows the children that playing at recess is important. In addition, when children have nice stuff to play with they do a better job of taking care of it.

Now What?

It's not easy turning your playground around so that problems are reduced, students learn valuable skills, and the school day runs smoothly. It takes commitment, dedication, and hard work from everyone involved. Now that you've finished reading the 6-Steps to a Trouble-free Playground it's time to move forward and make some changes. Change is always difficult so don't try to do too much at one time. Start with the underlying philosophy of this program. The schools that have implemented this program with dedication have been very successful. Other schools have failed because they weren't committed to the philosophy. Once you're committed to teaching self-responsibility, fostering intrinsic motivation, and using the inclusion style of teaching, you're ready to go. Remember, it's a journey that you're taking, not a destination you're trying to get to. Focus on the process of where you're taking students, not on the product of where they are.

When trying to implement the ideas presented in this book keep in mind it will be easier starting with the younger grades and working up than with the older grades and working down. Create change starting with grades K-2, then work your way up. You will always find resistance trying to work the other direction. It takes time. Be patient.

Recess is a fun time and a great learning tool. Keep in mind that over 90% of the children at your school think recess is the best part of the day. That right there should tell you how valuable recess is. Use it to help your students learn and grow.

If you need some ideas on games or activities for your playground, obtain a copy of my book, *Games Kids Should Play at Recess* (Hinson, 1997). It's filled with developmentally games and activities for every grade in elementary school. Also, if I can be of assistance to you please do not hesitate to contact me. I travel the country presenting this program to teachers and administrators. If you want information on my workshops, please contact me. Best of luck with your playground.

You can contact the author for book or workshop information at:

Curt Hinson, Ph.D.
237 Beau Tree Drive
Wilmington DE 19810
Phone 302-475-6025
Fax 302-475-3146

A mind once stretched by a new idea, never regains it original dimension.

— Oliver Wendell Holmes

References

Cantor, L. (1976). *Assertive Discipline: A take charge approach for today's educator.* Santa Monica, CA: Lee Cantor & Associates.

Goleman, D. (1995). *Emotional Intelligence: Why it can matter more than IQ.* New York: Bantam Books.

Hellison, D.R. (1995). *Teaching responsibility through physical activity.* Champaign, IL: Human Kinetics.

Hellison, D.R. (1985). *Goals and strategies for teaching physical education.* Champaign, IL: Human Kinetics.

Hinson, C. (1997). *Games kids should play at recess.* Wilmington, DE: PE Publishing Co.

Jensen, E. (1998). *Introduction to brain compatible learning.* San Diego: The Brain Store, Inc.

Jensen, E. (1997). *Brain compatible strategies.* San Diego: The Brain Store, Inc.

Kohn, A. (1993). *Punished by rewards: The trouble with gold stars, incentive plans, A's, praise, and other bribes.* New York: Houghton Mifflin Co.

Mosston, M., & Ashworth, S. (1990). *The spectrum of teaching styles: From command to discovery.* New York: Longman.

About the Author

Curt Hinson, Ph.D., taught elementary physical education in Wilmington, Delaware for 16 years. He holds a B.S. degree in health and physical education, a master's of education degree, and a Ph.D. in Kinesiology. Curt is also the author of *Fitness for Children* and *Games Kids Should Play at Recess*.

Curt was the 1992 NASPE Eastern District Elementary PE Teacher of the Year, and the 1991 Delaware Elementary PE Teacher of the Year. He has made presentations in over 40 states, and continues to tour the country sharing his knowledge on teaching and learning through play.

Curt enjoys cycling, jogging, weight training, reading, and watching his sons play baseball and ice hockey. He lives in Wilmington, Delaware with his wife, Michele, and their two sons, Taylor and Keegan.

Appendix A

The Levels of Behavior

Unacceptable (Level 1)
- Not following directions
- Not participating
- Arguing
- Hitting or pushing
- Out of control

Acceptable (Level 2)
- Following directions
- Participating
- Taking care of equipment
- Respectful of others
- Under control

Outstanding (Level 3)
- Being self-responsible
- Cooperating with others
- Returning equipment
- Helping others
- Acting as a role model

Appendix B

Playground Equipment List for the Elementary School Classroom

Mesh Equipment Bag	1
Football	1
Soccerball	1
Basketball	1
Aerobie Super Disc	2
Half cone	8
8' Jump Rope	2
9' Jump Rope	2
Hoops	3
Wiffleball Bat	1
Playground Ball	2
Softball-size Wiffleball	8
Beanbags	6
Pinky Sponge Ball	2

Most of the above equipment is available in variety of colors, which is helpful in determining what equipment belongs to what class. Be sure to purchase equipment that is developmentally appropriate for the grade level you're using it with. For example, younger grades need smaller, lighter, and softer versions of many of the above balls.

Appendix C

Recess Evaluation Form

1. What did you play at recess today?

2. Who did you play with?

3. At what level did you play?

    Level 1   Level 2   Level 3

4. What did you do that put you at that level?

Notes

Notes

Notes

Notes